W9-AYO-665

Why Do We Wear?

Hats and Headdresses
through History

by
Fiona MacDonald

GARETH**STEVENS**
GS
PUBLISHING
A Member of the WRC Media Family of Companies

Please visit our Web site at: www.garethstevens.com
For a free color catalog describing Gareth Stevens Publishing's
list of high-quality books and multimedia programs, call
1-800-542-2595 (USA) or 1-800-387-3178 (Canada).
Gareth Stevens Publishing's fax: (414) 332-3567.

Library of Congress Cataloging-in-Publication Data

McDonald, Fiona, 1942-
   Hats and headdresses through history / by Fiona McDonald.
      p. cm. — (Why do we wear?)
   Includes index.
   ISBN-10: 0-8368-6854-4 — ISBN-13: 978-0-8368-6854-8 (lib. bdg.)
   1. Headgear—History—Juvenile literature. I. Title. II. Series.
GT2110.M436   2007
391.4'3—dc22   2006015925

This North American edition first published in 2007 by
Gareth Stevens Publishing
A Member of the WRC Media Family of Companies
330 West Olive Street, Suite 100
Milwaukee, Wisconsin 53212 USA

This edition copyright © 2007 by Gareth Stevens, Inc. Original edition copyright © 2006
by ticktock Entertainment Ltd. First published in Great Britain by ticktock Media Ltd.,
Unit 2 Orchard Business Centre, North Farm Road, Tunbridge Wells, Kent TN2 3XF.

Managing editor: Valerie J. Weber
Gareth Stevens editor: Gini Holland
Gareth Stevens art direction: Tammy West
Gareth Stevens designer: Kami Strunsee

Picture Credits (t=top, b=bottom, l=left, r=right, c=center)
Alamy: 14t; Ancient Art and Architecture: 15t, 22-23; Bridgeman Art Library; 13 all;
CORBIS: 7t, 16t, 16-17, 18b, 19t, 27t; NASA; 27b; Rex Features: 25b;
ShutterstockRF: cover and 4b, 23t, 23b, 26 all, 28 all, 29 all;
ticktock Media Image Archive: 4t, 5t, 6t, 12 all, 14b, 15b, 20 all, 21 all, 22t, 24 all, 25t;
Werner Forman Archive: 7b, 8 all, 9 all, 10b 11t, 11b; World Religions: 5b, 6b, 17t, 17bl.

Every effort has been made to trace the copyright holders, and we apologize in advance for any unintentional omission.
We would be pleased to insert the appropriate acknowledgements in any subsequent edition of this publication.

Printed in the United States of America

1 2 3 4 5 6 7 8 9 10 09 08 07 06

Table of Contents

Cover: A model wears an elaborate hat, much like the styles seen at the Kentucky Derby.

Words that appear in the glossary are printed in
boldface type the first time they occur in the text.

Introduction

Why do we wear hats? We wear them for all sorts of reasons. Hats change the way we look. They frame our faces, hide our hair, and protect the most important part of our bodies — the brain!

Fashion and Survival

Many hats are decorative. We wear them for fun and for fashion. Hats may also tell people about a person's sense of style. The wrong hat spoils a great outfit, but the right hat helps create the perfect look. Other hats help us stay warm, safe, and dry. We rely on these hats to survive.

What Hats Say about You

Hats reveal something about your place in the world. Some large hats look important. Some fancy hats look rich. An old saying claims, "If you want to get ahead, get a hat!" Hats may also show what job you have. Hats can even tell people you are a boy or a girl. In some places, a woman's headgear may show whether she is single, married, or a widow.

Some characters are never seen without their hats. Writer Dr. Seuss created the "Cat in the Hat" in 1954.

Hats can be used to get people to look at you. This man is wearing a rainbow-colored **top hat** to stand out from the crowd.

PRETTY IN **INK**™

Belonging and Respect

Hats can say something about your religion. Hats can also show what group you belong to. People of many religions, including Muslims, Jews, and Sikhs, believe that covering the head shows respect to God. Sports fans often wear hats to show loyalty to groups, such as school or professional sports teams. Sports teams often wear hats or helmets with their team colors and logos, so fans can tell them apart.

Sikhs show respect for God by wearing turbans.

How much heat do we lose through our heads if we don't wear hats?

Protective Clothing

Hoods and head scarves keep our heads warm and dry. They shade us from hot sunshine. **Caps** and helmets protect us from dirt and danger. Helmets protect us in times of war. Helmets also protect us when we do sports such as skateboarding or biking. Caps protect eyes from too much sunlight.

This man's clothing is made to protect him when the wind blows dust across the desert.

The First Head Coverings

Some birds have feather crests. They fan them to attract mates. Male lions have big manes of hair. Early humans liked these animals, so they copied them. They made headdresses for powerful people. They hoped these would give their leaders some of the power of wild animals.

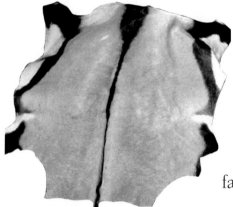

The First Hats

When were the first hats were made? Even scientists do not know. They do know that early humans lived over two million years ago. Early humans may have put animal skins over their heads to keep warm. Perhaps they shaded their faces from the Sun with mats of leaves or grass.

Animal skins such as this buffalo hide were used by early humans to make simple hats to keep them warm.

Traditional Headgear

Today, traditional cultures in the Amazon rain forest in South America and the South Pacific still wear hats that copy animals and birds. There, rulers and leaders continue to wear fur or feather headdresses on ceremonial occasions.

This tribal leader from the Ecuadorian rain forest is wearing a colorful feather headdress with matching rain forest flowers.

Garlands

In many parts of the world, women and girls follow another old custom. They make beautiful **garlands**, or chains, of delicate wild flowers to put in their hair. Flowers called daisies are often used to make daisy chains. Garlands are a good example of head coverings that are just decorative.

It takes patience and nimble fingers to make a daisy-chain.

How do we know that prehistoric people wore flower headdresses?

Fur Hats

By 100,000 years ago, men and women had learned to make tools that could cut furs and animal skins. They learned how to keep skins soft. They learned how to sew them together. They made simple tops and pants from skins and furs, and they probably made hats as well. Fur hats are warm, soft, and beautiful. They can be great protection against bad weather.

Warm fur hoods, like this one worn by an Inuit from Alaska, may have first been made 100,000 years ago.

Ancient Egypt and Its Neighbors

I n hot, dry, dusty ancient Egypt, keeping clean was very important. Being clean was a sign of religious purity. Ordinary people washed in the River Nile. Wealthy families had shower rooms, where slaves poured water over bathers standing below.

Short hair and frequent baths helped Egyptians stay cool in their hot climate.

Cool and Clean

To keep cool and clean, men and women shaved their heads or cut their hair very short. Children had their heads shaved, too, except for a strand left trailing beside one ear. This strand was called "the **lock** of youth."

Wigs for Dress Up

Rich men and women wore wigs made of human or animal hair. Some wore wigs because it was the fashion. Some wigs also covered up baldness. Styles changed over the years, from long **ringlets** or thick braids to short, tight curls. On special occasions, wigs might be decorated with beads and scented with perfume. Most ordinary people could not afford fancy wigs. They sometimes wore rough wigs made of plant fiber. Some wore simple cloth wigs.

This wig of curled, braided human hair was made in about 1500 B.C.

An Everyday Crown

Ancient Egyptian statues, carvings, and tomb paintings often show **pharaohs** wearing a **pschent**, or double **crown**. This crown was a symbol of the two separate regions of Egypt, united in about 3100 B.C. The top of the crown was white, representing Upper (southern) Egypt. The lower part was red, signifying Lower (northern) Egypt.

This tomb model shows King Tutankhamun wearing the "war crown" of the pharaohs.

c. 3000 B.C. – 500 B.C.

This seventh century B.C. Nubian King wears a diadem.

The Sign of a King

Royal crowns and headdresses were usually decorated with a fierce cobra. The cobra was the symbol of the goddess Wadjet. Wadjet was a special protector of kings. In neighboring Nubia, rulers wore **diadems** on top of short hair. The royal diadem was also decorated with images of cobras.

What type of hat was shown in a cave in Thebes?

A bust, thought to be of King Amenemhat IV, shows the pharaoh wearing the "**nemes**" headcloth with a **uraeus**.

9

Ancient Greece and Rome

The Ancient Greeks believed that the head was the home of the soul. Greek head coverings had practical uses and also showed the person's moral worth. Clothing in ancient Greece was usually a simple linen top, but hairstyles, particularly for women, were very fancy. The ancient Romans had their own styles. They took many fashions from their neighbors in Greece, but sometimes, they invented new styles of their own.

Men

Many Greek men went bare-headed most of the time. Bare heads showed they had nothing to hide. Citizens of democratic states, they felt proud and free. When it rained, they wore **pesatos**, which are hats with wide **brims**, or pulled cloaks over their heads. Athletes tied their hair back with ribbons to keep it out of their eyes.

Garlands for Men

Roman emperors also wore garlands, but their garlands were not made of flowers. They were made of laurel leaves. When they marched in victory parades, Roman generals were "crowned" with laurel leaves. Roman writers said that laurels represented peace, joy, and victory. A laurel is an evergreen tree. It was sacred to Jupiter, the most powerful Roman god, so the laurel was also a symbol of strength.

Headgear for Soldiers

In wartime, Greek soldiers wore helmets to protect their heads from enemy swords and spears. Each soldier had to buy his own helmet. Cheap helmets were made of tough, boiled leather. Soldiers from poor families could only afford leather helmets. Better, stronger helmets were made from sheets of bronze that were hammered into shape. Rich soldiers could buy bronze helmets. Designs often included nose guards, cheek guards, and tall crests on top.

Crests like these on copies of Roman army helmets helped soldiers find friends in battle.

Military Headgear

Roman soldiers wore helmets like ancient Greek ones, but they added new parts. Their battle helmets had moving **visors**. Their helmets also had cheek guards that they could take off and put back on. Romans added a curved rim to protect the back of the neck. Helmets worn on parade might be decorated with metal. Some parade helmets had brightly colored crests made of feathers or horsehair.

This helmet was made from a single piece of bronze. It would have been worn by a **hoplite** (citizen foot-soldier) from the city-state of Athens.

Women

Greek men expected women to cover their hair with **veils**. Beneath these veils, women arranged their long hair in elaborate braids, curls, and buns. Women's hairstyles were held in place by colored scarves or ribbons. They also used jeweled hairpins or diadems. Ancient Greek jewelers were highly skilled at working with gold.

Roman Veils

Like the Greeks, Roman women covered their heads with veils. They chose different colors and styles for different events. They wore red veils to weddings to scare away evil spirits. Brides added garlands of wild flowers and wore cone-shaped hairstyles with their veils.

What was the prize given to the first Olympic champions?

This gold diadem (*left*) from the island of Milos, for a woman's hair, dates from 300 B.C. Julia Titi, daughter of Titus, is shown here (*right*) in a curly blond wig.

Medieval Europe

Soon after A.D. 300, Roman power grew weak. Roman lands were lost to many different peoples. Languages and customs changed. Different peoples settled in different parts of Europe. Their clothing changed into different styles. Hats and headgear changed, too.

> To give thanks to God, Visigoth kings hung their crowns in Spanish Christian churches.

Visigoths

In about A.D. 500, **Visigoths** from northeast Europe took control of land in Italy and Spain. They were led by warlike kings, who wore wide, band-shaped crowns of gold **latticework**, studded with precious stones and hung with jingling gold pendants. Gradually, circlets of gold and jewels replaced Roman laurel leaf garlands as symbols of royal status in south European lands.

Local Headgear

In the Middle Ages, or medieval times, married women throughout Europe continued to cover their heads with veils or shawls. Local climate and farming practices shaped the wide variety in men's headgear. In hot, sunny Italy, for example, men's hats had wide, shady brims. In cold, snowy lands, like Russia and Scandinavia, men wore hats made of bushy fox fur. In wet, windy Britain, they continued to wear Celtic-style hoods.

> This Italian farm worker is wearing a wide-brimmed hat made from locally grown wheat-straw that was braided and stitched together.

Battle Helmets

Men's battle helmets also showed local traditions. Viking and Anglo-Saxon helmets that had been made before A.D. 1000 were decorated with monsters from pagan myths and legends. Their basic shape was a simple dome, and they were designed to be worn with chain mail armor. After about 1300, fashions in helmets changed to suit new styles of plate armor. Metal helmets enclosed the whole head and had to be specially made to fit each person.

The Pope was leader of all Christians in medieval Europe. What was his tall hat called?

This fifteenth-century Dutch illustration shows people wearing elaborate hats.

Women's Hats

About the same time, rich women began to wear hats instead of simple veils. At first, their hats were based on male designs. After about 1400, women's fashions included tall, pointed hennins (steeple-hats); wide, padded hats with horns; and **gable** headdresses that formed a pointed frame around the face.

Asia

any different peoples of Asia and Arabia all had their own customs and traditions, which were reflected in their clothes. They lived in many environments and followed several of the world's great faiths. These factors also affected what they chose to wear.

Religious Head Coverings

The Muslim faith encourages men and women to dress modestly. Many Muslims believe this means keeping the head covered in public at all times. In the Muslim homelands of Western Asia, men wore the traditional desert head covering: a **kaffiyeh**, a cotton square folded into a triangle. Muslim women covered their hair with veils or with a fold of their long cloaks, called *abayahs*. Some wore burkas, which are cloaks that completely covers the head, face, and body. Many Muslims still wear these traditional head coverings today.

The traditional Arab kaffiyeh shades the head and protects the neck from sunburn.

Warm Wool and Fur

In Central Asia, where the weather is colder and wetter, men and women wore **pillbox**-shaped woolen caps. In winter, men covered their caps with fur hats, while women tied on head scarves. Turkish men wore a tall, cone-shaped cap of wool **felt**, called a fez. Turkish women kept their heads warm with head scarves and shawls.

A traditional fez, worn in Turkey, was made of red felt.

What is another word for a fez?

Muslim scholars wore turbans, shown here in about A.D. 1350. Many Muslims and Sikhs still wear turbans today.

Pillboxes and Turbans

In many parts of India and Southeast Asia, **turbans**, which are long strips of cloth wound around the head, were the usual headgear for men. Women draped the ends of their saris — wrapped cloth dresses that end in a long scarf — or long, wide *dupattas*, or head scarves, over their hair. For work in the rice fields, farmers throughout Southeast Asia made shady, waterproof hats of tough local materials, such as bamboo or woven palm fronds.

China

Chinese hairstyles showed the wearer's rank and occupation. Men grew their hair long and covered it with black head scarves. Scholars and government officials topped their head scarves with black hats that had folding side panels. Army leaders wore helmets trimmed with feathers.

This model Japanese emperor wears a *kammuri* (tall black silk hat). His empress has an elaborate *suberakashi* hairstyle and a chrysanthemum crest.

Farm laborers in southern China wore wide, cone-shaped bamboo hats. Chinese women tied their long hair into neat buns. It was not respectable to let hair flow freely. Outside their homes, high-ranking women wore veils. Clothing styles in Japan and Korea were influenced by China, their powerful neighbor.

Africa

Traditionally, African men and women wore a wide range of headgear. It was made in different styles and materials, depending on the local environment and resources. African hairstyles followed traditional local designs, each with their own meaning. Typically, styles included braids, hairpins, decorative combs, feathers, and colored clay.

Traditionally, the Tuareg men of Morocco wore veils dyed deep blue with indigo. In Sudan, white veils were popular.

Dressed for the Desert

Men and women living in or around the vast, sandy Sahara Desert needed headgear that would protect them from heat, dust, sandstorms, and sunburn. They covered their heads and the lower part of their faces with long strips of cloth, wound around and around. Men's styles looked like turbans with a wide cloth strip added to protect the mouth and nose. Women's styles were simpler, much like shawls, and covered the whole face.

Caps and Crowns

In West Africa, short, close-cropped hairstyles were popular among men and some women. Ordinary people wore caps and head ties. Powerful West African kings and queens wore elaborate crowns and headdresses made of coral or colorful beads. Some crowns showed portraits of ancestors. Others made royal wearers look taller than ordinary people.

This Queen Inyang Inyang statue from Nigeria dates from about 1610 to 1620.

Married Beauty

In many parts of Africa, young, unmarried girls went bare headed. Covering the hair was a sign of being married. In regions where fine cloth was produced, especially West Africa, married women traditionally wore head wraps, scarves, or ties. These were large squares or long lengths of patterned fabric that were folded and tied in pleasing arrangements. Simple wraps were worn by ordinary women. High, wide, complicated head ties were a sign of wealth and status. They were worn by women who did little manual work.

A simple head scarf is worn by a young woman from Algeria.

Herero women from Namibia in traditional *duk* hats.

Signs of Belonging

Many hats were worn, by men and women, to show that they belonged to one particular group. Sometimes, headgear was a sign of tribal or national identity. For example, the Herero women of Namibia still wear high, wide hats, called *duk*, made of tightly-wrapped cloth. Sometimes, headgear displayed rank or bravery. Warriors from the Zulu people of South Africa wore plumes of ostrich feathers. Masai warriors (in what is now Kenya) colored their hair with orange-colored mud and arranged it in braids. Headdresses were often an important part of ceremonial costumes that masked dancers and priests wore in ceremonies.

Why were women's head wraps useful as well as attractive?

17

Early Americas

The continents of North and South America cover a vast area and have many different climate zones and environments. Using local materials, native peoples living on these continents developed a wide range of headgear designed to suit local conditions.

Fantastic Feathers

Feathers were used to make ceremonial headgear in many parts of North and South America. Usually, there were strict laws about who could wear them. The finest feathers were kept for royal rulers. In Mexico, Aztec artists also showed them in headdresses worn by gods. Feathers were also awarded like medals to brave warriors.

This warrior from a Native American tribe is wearing a headdress of red feathers.

In the Cold

In the frozen Arctic, the Inuit and Aleut peoples made cozy hooded parkas and anoraks from seal skin and fox fur. In tropical Central America, Mayan people created headdresses out of brightly colored cloth, skillfully woven from local plant fibers and decorated with embroidery. In the high Andes Mountains of South America, Inca artisans spun and wove soft, warm llama fleece to make hats with earflaps for protection against frostbite.

This musician from Peru wears a modern version of an ancient Inca hat design.

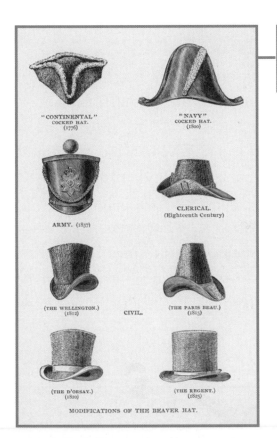

North American Indian style

Different tribes decorated their heads in very different ways. Some North American warriors shaved their heads. Others, such as the Sac and Fox, left a strip of hair standing tall in the center of their heads. This style was later called a "Mohican." Many Central American women arranged their hair on either side of their faces in circular **squash blossom** shapes or pinned braids on top their heads to create "horns."

Sac (or Sauk) Indian Chief Keokuk wears what was later called a "Mohican."

How many birds were killed to make an Aztec feather headdress?

Beaver hats provided protection against the elements for European settlers.

"CONTINENTAL" COCKED HAT. (1776)

"NAVY" COCKED HAT. (1800)

ARMY. (1837)

CLERICAL. (Eighteenth Century)

(THE WELLINGTON.) (1812)

CIVIL.

(THE PARIS BEAU.) (1815)

(THE D'ORSAY.) (1820)

(THE REGENT.) (1825)

MODIFICATIONS OF THE BEAVER HAT.

European Settlers

After 1492, European explorers and settlers arrived in the Americas. They brought European headgear with them. After about 1600, tall black hats made of wool felt or compressed beaver fur were popular for men. Women wore thick cloth hoods on top of white cloth **bonnets** that tied under the chin. Hoods were often lined with fur purchased from Native American trappers.

Europe 1500 - 1700

In Europe, the years from 1500 to 1750 were exciting but troubled times. Explorers brought new products from distant lands. Teachers, preachers, and artists challenged old ideas. Headgear became some of the richest ever seen in Europe.

Bonnets

Bonnets (wide flat caps without peaks) were first worn by teachers and their pupils. Then many fashionable men chose to wear them as well. They trimmed their rich black silk velvet caps with imported feathers or pearls.

A group of Tudor boys dressed in bonnets.

Fancy Caps and Ruffs

Fashionable women copied styles worn by powerful queens and princesses. The French hood (a crescent-shaped, jeweled cap worn on top of a hood which covered most of the hair) was popular throughout Europe. So were neck ruffs, which were wide bands of pleated linen that first came from Spain. Ruffs framed the face and were also worn by men. Poor people could not afford these fancy fashions. Poor men wore woolen bonnets, while poor women wore head scarves and shawls.

This woman wears a French hood.

After 1620

About 1620, styles changed. Fashionable men and women wore long ringlets tumbling over their shoulders and wide-brimmed hats made of felt, beaver hair, or leather. Strict Protestants (sometimes called Puritans) believed that such fancy styles were ungodly. Puritan men wore close-cropped hair. Puritan women wore neat buns and plain, white linen caps.

1500 – 1750

A group of English men, in about 1610, wear typical wide-brimmed hats.

After 1680

By about 1680, natural hair was replaced by long, curled wigs. Men topped these with big tricorne (three-cornered) hats. Women wore frontlets, or lace headdresses stiffened by wire, with trailing ribbons that were called lappets. By about 1750, women's wigs had become outrageously high. They were padded with wool and decorated with flowers and feathers. In contrast, men's wigs were smaller, with neat short curls and a little ponytail, called a queue, which is French for *tail*.

This drawing of a wealthy woman shows her wearing a tall headdress.

Western World 1750-1900

Between 1750 and 1900, the western world — Europe, the Americas, and some European colonies — changed more quickly than ever before. New styles were mass produced and shown in the world's first fashion magazines, printed in France. Workers' hats remained plain and practical.

These small hats that decorate hair date from the 1850s.

Greek Influence

From about 1780 to 1810, fashions were based on ancient Greek designs. Men and women mostly went bare headed. Men had short hair. Women also cut their hair or wore long locks swept up in the Greek style.

New Romantics

By 1820, new "romantic" fashions were popular for women. These featured shady **picture hats**, or bonnets with wide brims that framed the woman's face. Underneath, women tied their hair neatly into buns. Beginning in about 1870, women took off their big bonnets and put on small hats, worn tilting forward. Now, they had room for fancy hairstyles with **chignons**, or ringlets at the back.

Children were dressed like miniature adults. This girl is wearing a large straw picture hat, tied with a wide ribbon.

Men's Fashions

About 1850, many new hat styles were introduced for men. A hard, dome-shaped, felt hat with a narrow brim became very popular. It was named after its designer, William Bowler. In the United States, people called it a **derby**. Another new style was a light, flat-crowned straw **boater**, for boating and summertime wear. The **homburg**, a warm, wide-brimmed felt hat, was named after the German town where it was first made. Men had their hair cut short and neat, but long, bushy side-whiskers were very fashionable.

The **bowler** hat became the traditional headgear of London businessmen.

These classic stetson hats kept cowboys cool during their working days.

In the United States

In the U.S., new hats were designed to meet new working conditions. Trappers and hunters in the north woods wore fur caps, often decorated with animal tails. Cowboys riding across hot, dusty prairies wore cool, wide-brimmed, high-crowned stetsons. Housewives and female farm workers shaded their faces with big cotton sunbonnets.

Why did people think hatters were mad?

Late nineteenth-century styles stayed popular at the start of the twentieth century. Waving, upswept hair was still seen as a woman's "crowning glory." To show off their hair, women's hats were still small, highly decorated, and not at all practical. Men still wore the old top hats, bowlers, and homburgs. They also liked sporting styles, such as the **deerstalker** cap and the felt hat.

World War I

The start of World War I in 1914 changed fashions forever. Men wore military uniform hats and helmets or practical caps. Women wore neat, simple hats or headgear linked to their wartime duties, such as nurses caps and veils, or head scarves and hairnets when they worked in weapons factories.

FIVE THOUSAND BY JUNE

GRADUATE NURSES YOUR COUNTRY NEEDS YOU

This World War I poster shows a nurse wearing a simple nurse's cap.

The Cloche Hat

After the war ended in 1918, women refused to return to their earlier way of life — or style of clothing. They cut their hair and experimented with the world's first permanent waves. They wore tight-fitting cloche (bell-shaped) hats with tiny brims, pulled low down over the face.

Cloche hats of the 1920s were plain, simple, and easy to wear. They would fit only over simple hairstyles.

Menswear

Flat cloth caps — sometimes large and baggy — were still popular with working men. They were also worn by people when they played sports such as golf. For daytime wear, country men often wore tweed caps. City dwellers chose a soft, wide-brimmed felt hat, called a **trilby** or a **fedora**, for informal wear, but stylish businessmen preferred a bowler hat or very formal top hat.

The flat cap was worn by people of all classes and a variety of sportsmen around the world.

What was an opera hat?

World War II

A second terrible world war, World War II, which lasted from 1939 to 1945, saw men and women wearing uniform headgear. Off-duty, choice of hats was limited by severe shortages of fabric and trimmings. Styles were small, neat, and inspired by uniforms.

Men and women in the U.S. armed forces during World War II wore camouflaged helmets. Here, John Wayne portrays a soldier.

25

Western World 1950–2000

I n the late twentieth century, for the first time in thousands of years, most men and women in the Western world stopped wearing hats as part of their everyday clothing. For several years after the end of World War II in 1945, however, hats continued to be part of both formal and everyday dress for men and women.

Special occasions

Older people wore hats for special occasions, such as weddings and funerals, and for church services. Women's hat designs could be anything from tiny "pillboxes" to big, floppy, floral styles. Men's styles remained largely unchanged from earlier in the century.

A model today wears a 1960s-style pillbox hat as part of a wedding outfit.

Für sportliches Fahren
auf Sonderwunsch mit Sporttüren aus Leichtmetall und Sportscheibe

Zur weiteren Gewichtsverminderung können die Stoßstangen und auch das Verdeck abgeschraubt werden

Sports cars made the concept of hat wearing unfashionable.

Out of Fashion?

New technologies — such as central heating and warm, comfortable car travel — made hats less necessary. People did not need as much protection from bad weather. New ideas also made hats unfashionable, especially among the young. They said hats were out-of-date, silly, and unattractive. To them, hats just seemed fussy and usually messed up their hair.

Changing Hairstyles

Hairstyles remained important, however. Beginning in the 1960s, waist-length flowing hair (for men as well as women) mocked neat, tidy 1940s fashions. Often, hair was dyed with henna imported from India. Bushy "Afro" curls and dreadlocks became a way for people of African descent to show pride in their identity as they demanded equal civil rights.

Rastafarian men grew long dreadlocks and wore knitted **tams** to show that they were followers of the religion. Tams can hold a mass of dreadlocks.

1950 – 2000

Hats for Work

Work was the only place where hats were worn more often than in the past. New laws protected workers, so new materials, such as shatterproof plastics, were used to improve safety headgear. Astronauts who took part in United States and Soviet Russian space exploration flights needed specially designed helmets to survive beyond Earth's atmosphere.

Space helmets gave astronauts air to breathe. They also helped remove waste products.

Global Styles Today

Today, in the early years of the twenty-first century, fashions have become global, or worldwide. TV, the Internet, and other forms of communication take only seconds to bring images of the latest styles from all over the world. International corporations have factories making designs in many different countries. They sell them wherever they can find customers.

Workers' Headgear

Staying with twentieth century fashions, many men, women, and children never wear a hat. Headgear is still worn by many workers, however. Hospital staff wear caps, masks, and hairnets to keep their workplaces clean. Laborers, police, firefighters, and soldiers all wear strong headgear. Tourists who visit hot, sunny countries are told to protect their skin with large, shady hats and sunscreen.

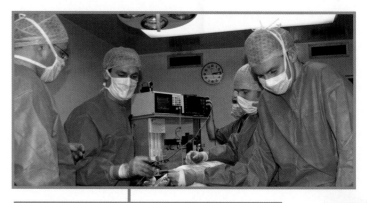

Hospital surgeons wear surgical masks and hairnets to keep the operating room free of germs.

Sports and Leisure

A skateboarder wears a protective helmet while making a dramatic jump.

Professional sports stars wear strong helmets decorated with team colors and sponsors' logos. Other sportswear styles, such as baseball caps or pull-on knitted hats, are popular leisure wear, especially for young people. Like hooded tops, they can be both a fashion statement and a sign of belonging to a peer group.

Men of the Orthodox Hasidic Jewish community, founded in the eighteenth century, still wear round-brimmed black hats.

Religion

For people who follow older traditions, hats are still important. Many Jewish men choose to wear a **yarmulke** (skullcap) as a sign of respect for God. Muslim women and girls wear several different styles of head-covering, called *hijab*, or modest dress. Many Sikh and Muslim men also cover their heads. Elaborate head scarves and braided hairstyles are valued African traditions.

What is the most popular hat in the world today?

Today's teens wear all kinds of hats, including baggy corduroy caps.

Fashion Now

Some people wear hats just because hats make them feel good. Fashion designers dress top models in hats at fashion shows. Some of the world's most famous people choose fancy hats for important public appearances. These days, people of all ages like to wear baseball caps. Boys and girls, men and women wear them backward, forward, or to the side. Around the world, hats of all shapes, sizes, and colors are always on parade.

Glossary

boater hat made of stiff, braided straw with a flat crown and a narrow brim.

bonnet for women, a hood-shaped hat, often with a ruffle or lace-trimmed brim, that fastens under the chin. For men, a baggy cap, with or without a brim

bowler hat with a narrow curved brim and a hard, dome-shaped crown, also known as a derby

brim the lower edge of the hat that sticks out from the crown

cap (men) a small, neat hat without a brim or a hat shaped like an upside-down bowl, with a stiff, small brim in front

cap (women) a small, neat hat without a brim, or a small bonnet, made of lace or another thin, delicate material

chignon long hair twisted into a loose knot, pinned up at the back of the head

crown the part of a hat that covers the top of the head. For royal people, crowns are open-topped hats, shaped like headbands, usually made of metal and highly decorated, often with jewels

deerstalker a cap made of thick warm cloth, with flaps to cover the ears

derby a hat with a narrow curved brim and a hard, dome-shaped crown, also known as a bowler

diadem decorative headband

fedora soft felt hat with a wide brim — also known as a trilby

felt thick cloth made of boiled wool or animal hair.

gable pointed part of a roof, used to describe a headdress worn by women in sixteenth-century Europe

garland circle of leaves or flowers that can be worn for decoration either on the head or around the neck

hijab modest dress worn by Muslims, often used to describe a head scarf worn by Muslim women

homburg soft felt hat for men, first made in Homburg, Germany

hoplite citizen foot soldier who served in ancient Greece

kaffiyeh cloth headdress worn by men in Arab countries of North Africa and the Middle East

latticework crisscross framework or network of crossed strips

lock trailing strand of hair, often curled

nemes striped cloth headdress, worn in ancient Egypt

pesatos wide-brimmed leather hat worn in ancient Greece

pharaohs kings who ruled ancient Egypt and were entombed in pyramids

picture hat woman's hat with a wide soft brim that frames the face — often decorated with flowers and ribbons

pillbox small, round, flat-topped hat without a brim, named after round boxes that used to contain pills

pschent double crown, worn by pharaohs of Ancient Egypt

ringlets long, tight, trailing curls

squash blossom big, wide-open flowers of plants belonging to the squash (pumpkin) family

tam a loose, usually knit, baggy cap. These caps, worn by Scots men in the nineteenth century, were first called "Tam O'Shanters," after the hero in a poem by the Scots author, Robert Burns.

top hat men's hat with a very tall, flat-topped crown

trilby soft felt hat with a wide brim, also known as a fedora

turban a long strip of cloth wrapped around the head, worn by men in Asia and by male followers of the Sikh religion

uraeus a cobra, head raised and ready to strike, which was a symbol of kingship and divine protection in ancient Egypt

Visigoths tribes from northern Europe who migrated to Italy and Spain soon after A.D. 500

veil thin cloth or netting that partly hides the face and hair

visor face covering that is part of a battle helmet or other protective headgear

yarmulke skull cap worn by Jewish men

Answers

Page 5: up to 85 percent
Page 7: traces of flower pollen have been found in prehistoric graves, suggesting that garlands were worn
Page 9: a conical straw hat
Page 11: a garland of leaves from holy trees
Page 13: a tiara
Page 15: a tarboosh
Page 17: they cushioned the head when carrying heavy loads
Page 19: at least one hundred
Page 21: a French hood
Page 23: chemicals (especially mercury) used to make felt hats often damaged hatters' brains
Page 25: a collapsible top hat worn by men in formal evening dress for outings to the theater
Page 27: moon dust! NASA scientists believed that this was very explosive, too!
Page 29: the baseball cap

Index